GO THE BARK TO WORK

BARK TWAIN

V!VA
EDITIONS

Published in the United States by Viva Editions, an imprint of Start Midnight, LLC, 221 River Street, Ninth Floor, Hoboken, New Jersey 07030.

Printed in the United States

Trade paper ISBN: 978-1-63228-080-0

E-book ISBN: 978-1-63228-137-1

BARK TWAIN is a dog who knows his mind and is frustrated with the world today. His owner is just home too darn much.

After puppy school and watching all those tv shows with Cesar Millan, he is well trained, but his patience is running out with his owner. He admires the fame and fortune won by dogs like Snoopy, Lassie, and Clifford the Big Red Dog.

Bark Twain is thinking about buying Dogecoin, getting a Tesla, and flying to space on one of Elon Musk's SpaceX flights.

He is no fan of Grumpy Cat or Garfield. This is his first book.

ACKNOWLEDGMENTS

I'd like to thank everyone who worked on this book. Starting with Pablo, whose illustrations are unbelievable. Darren and his team at TidalWave Productions, for their great execution. Rene, for the great editing. Keith, Michael, Ashley, Meghan, Ron, and Jennifer for helping make this book a reality.

It's Monday morning,
and you're staying home,
so I get lots of treats
and really big bones.

Fifteen days have passed,
and you've been home for a while.
Please go back to work—
you're cramping my style.

GO THE BARK TO WORK!

6

I'm trying to cuddle with my girlfriend,
the hot poodle next door,
before she leaves me for the neighbor's Labrador.

GO THE BARK TO WORK!

You adopted me when I was only a pup.
Watching after you now,
I feel like I'm the grown-up.

You play video games all day.
You're always in a bad mood.
Go back to work so you can afford dog food.

GO THE BARK TO WORK!

Shouldn't you be at work,
adding to your wealth?
Your being home is bad
for my mental health.

GO THE BARK TO WORK!

14

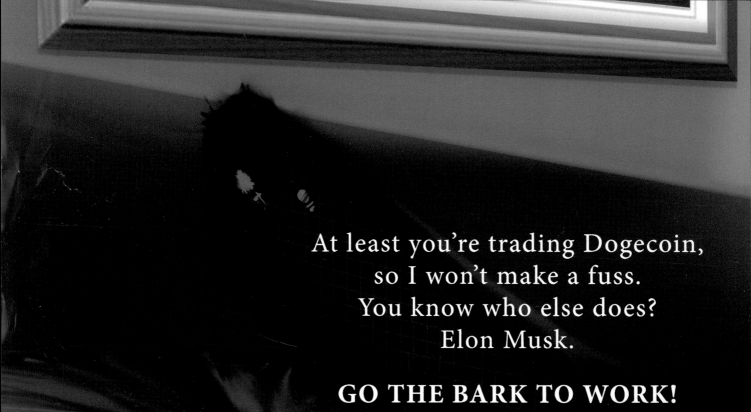

At least you're trading Dogecoin,
so I won't make a fuss.
You know who else does?
Elon Musk.

GO THE BARK TO WORK!

Now you're gaining weight daily—
go jog for fitness.
You're the reason food delivery
will never go out of business.

18

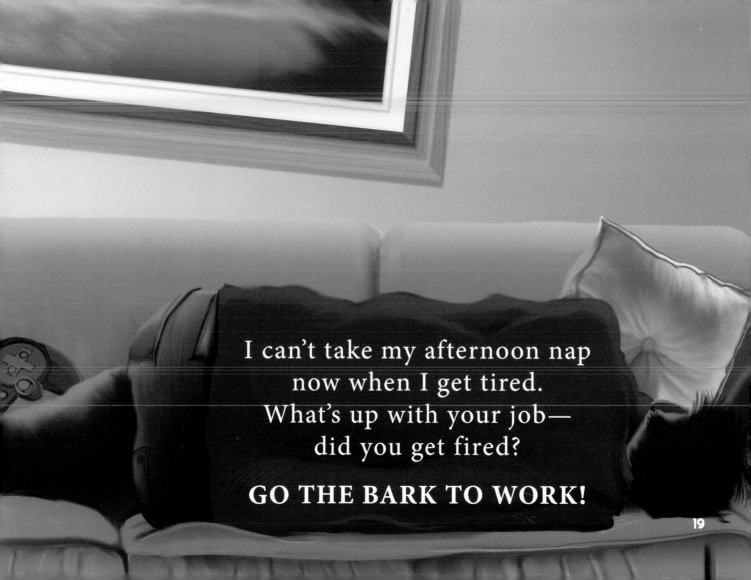

I can't take my afternoon nap now when I get tired. What's up with your job— did you get fired?

GO THE BARK TO WORK!

19

You watch porn all night,
and you're such a slob.
Here's the classified ads,
go find a job.

GO THE BARK TO WORK!

20

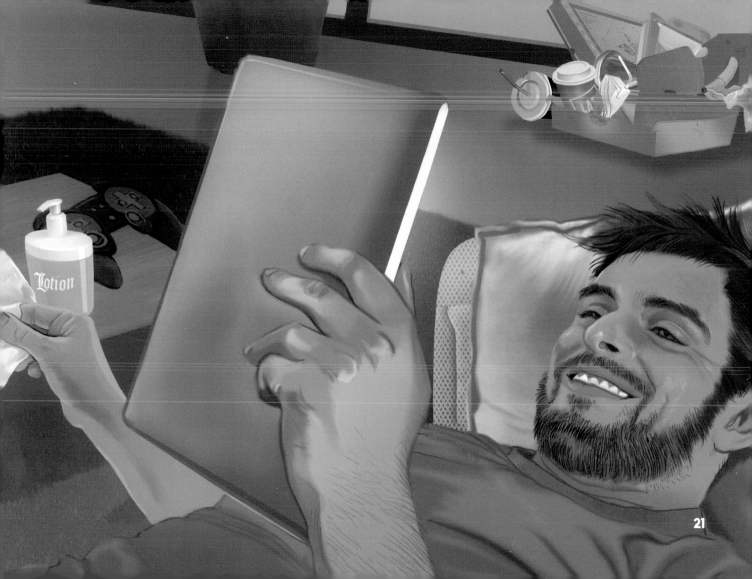

Lotion

21

23

If you would shave,
I would feel a lot calmer.
You're starting to look
like the Unabomber.

24

Fleas, ticks, or worms.
I'm not sure which I'll catch sooner.
You need to get your ass
to my groomer.

GO THE BARK TO WORK!

25

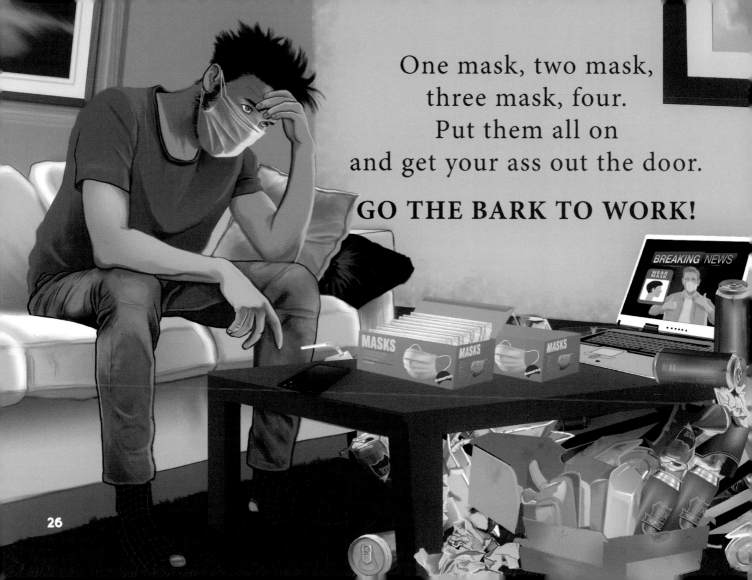

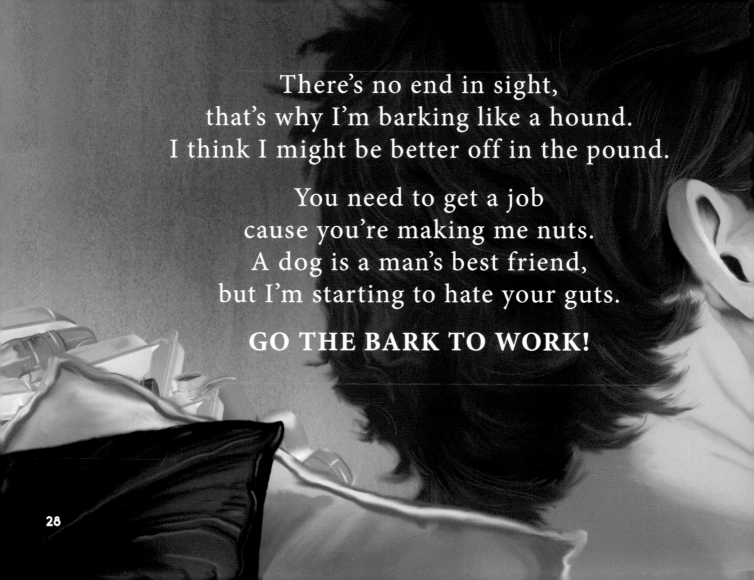

There's no end in sight,
that's why I'm barking like a hound.
I think I might be better off in the pound.

You need to get a job
cause you're making me nuts.
A dog is a man's best friend,
but I'm starting to hate your guts.

GO THE BARK TO WORK!

LAST 3 HRS

34,509,00

JOBS REPORT
10 MILLION JOB OPENINGS

29